Kindle Fire HD8 Tablet

How to Use Kindle Fire HD 8, the Complete User Guide with Step-by-Step Instructions, Tutorial to Unlock the True Potential of Your Device in 30 Minutes

MARK HOWARD

Table of Contents

INTRODUCTION	**11**
CHAPTER 1: INITIAL SETUP	**15**
Charge Your Device	15
Link Your Amazon Account	17
Register Your Device	19
Set Up Your Email	21
Transfer Your Media	23
CHAPTER 2: USING YOUR FIRE HD 8	**29**
Navigating Fire HD 8 Hardware	30
Basic Features on Your Device	35
Downloading Apps and Games	38
Alexa Hands-Free Starter Guide	39
CHAPTER 3: READING AND LISTENING	**45**
Buying and Downloading Kindle Content	46
Reading Your eBooks	48

Listening to Your Audiobooks	49
Reading Settings	50
Bookmarking, Highlights, and Note Taking	54
Listening to Music	56
Watching Movies	57
Amazon Memberships for Inexpensive Reading and Listening	58

CHAPTER 4: CUSTOMIZING YOUR SETTINGS 61

Change Your Background	61
Recommendations	63
Show New Items on Home Page	64
Change Home Page Navigation	66
Wi-Fi Connection	67
Bluetooth Mode	69
Device Options	70
Sounds and Notifications	71
Keyboard and Language	73
Accessibility Features	74
Undoing a Customized Feature	75

CHAPTER 5: SECURITY FEATURES 77

Lock Screen Passwords 78

Parental Controls 80

CHAPTER 6: TROUBLESHOOTING GUIDE 85

Unresponsive Touch Screen 86

Issues Purchasing and Accessing Content 88

Not Seeing Previously Purchased or Downloaded Content 91

App-Specific Issues 92

Battery Won't Charge / Won't Hold a Charge 97

Forgot Lock Screen Password 100

The Device is Not Playing Sound 100

Wi-Fi Not Connecting 106

Blue Hue around Edges of Screen 108

CHAPTER 7: ACCESSORIES 109

Cases 110

Kick Stands 112

Screen Protectors 113

CONCLUSION 115

CHECK OUT OTHER BOOKS   **117**

Text Copyright © Mark Howard

All rights reserved. No part of this guide may be reproduced in any form without permission in writing from the publisher except in the case of brief quotations embodied in critical articles or reviews.

Legal & Disclaimer

The information contained in this book and its contents is not designed to replace or take the place of any form of medical or professional advice; and is not meant to replace the need for independent medical, financial, legal or other professional advice or services, as may be required. The content and information in this book has been provided for educational and entertainment purposes only.

The content and information contained in this book has been compiled from sources deemed reliable, and it is accurate to the best of the Author's knowledge, information and belief. However, the Author cannot guarantee its accuracy and validity and cannot be held liable for any errors and/or omissions. Further, changes are periodically made to this book as and when needed. Where appropriate and/or necessary, you must consult a professional (including but not limited to your doctor, attorney, financial advisor or such other professional advisor) before using any of the suggested remedies, techniques, or information in this book.

Upon using the contents and information contained in this book, you agree to hold harmless the Author from and against any damages, costs, and expenses, including any legal fees potentially resulting from the application of any of the information provided by this book. This disclaimer applies to any loss, damages or injury caused by the use and application, whether directly or indirectly, of any advice or information presented, whether for breach of contract, tort, negligence, personal injury, criminal intent, or under any other cause of action.

You agree to accept all risks of using the information presented inside this book.

You agree that by continuing to read this book, where appropriate and/or necessary, you shall consult a professional (including but not limited to your doctor, attorney, or financial advisor or such other advisor as needed) before using any of the suggested remedies, techniques, or information in this book.

Introduction

Congratulations on purchasing your brand new Kindle Fire HD 8!

This device is a handy tablet that can support you in all types of things from consuming content to playing games and keeping track of your schedule. There are many great features built into the Kindle Fire HD 8.

The book "*Fire HD 8*" was designed to support you in understanding your device, navigating the hardware and software, and getting the most out of your experience. From supporting you in understanding the various applications and features to showing you how to access and manage customizable settings and security features, this book features everything you need to get the most out of your device.

Whether you have purchased your device for easy listening, movie watching, book reading, entertainment, personal management, or all of the above, you have come to the right place! This book will support you in having the best experience with your device possible. It is organized in a way that makes it easy to read and understand. You will receive direct and to-the-point step-by-step guides, all the way from helping you properly set up your brand new device to refrain from experiencing any issues, to troubleshooting anything you may face along the way.

This book has an emphasis on its troubleshooting chapter, making it an incredibly handy go-to guide to have available during your experience with your Fire HD 8 tablet. That way, if you run into any issues, you can quickly refer to this guide and receive access to the support you need. Due to the nature of technology, troubles are sometimes inevitable. Fortunately, the Fire HD 8 tablet has been out long enough that we know virtually everything you may run into and we can offer you excellent support in overcoming any troubles so you can continue enjoying your experience!

If you are ready, begin reading! Be sure to keep this book handy in case you need to reference it to receive support in your Kindle Fire HD 8 experience. And of course, enjoy.

Chapter 1: Initial Setup

Setting up your new Kindle Fire HD 8 is an extremely easy process. There are a few things that you will need to do in order to be ready to actually begin using your device. In this chapter, we will go over it step-by-step to make sure that you set your device up properly so that you can get the most out of it. Make sure to do this before anything else.

Charge Your Device

Inside of the box that your device comes in, you will find a charging cable and a brick. It is a good idea to connect the charging cable to the brick and charge your device from a wall outlet.

While you can charge it from a computer, this charge will take significantly longer to complete. If your Fire HD 8 is completely dead, it will not power on. You may see an empty battery cell with a small red line at the bottom indicating that the battery on your device has died. Once you begin charging it, the device should automatically turn back on once it has enough charge. However, if the device was already off when the battery died, it may stay off until you turn it back on. To check and see that your battery is fully charged, turn your device back on and swipe down from the top of the screen. There, your quick start menu will pop up. You can then look to the battery indicator and see if it is full or not. If it is, your battery is fully charged and you are good to go.

The Kindle Fire HD 8 comes with a micro USB charger. If you ever find that your charger is no longer working, you can replace the charger with any conventional micro USB cable. However, if you find that a generic branded one is not working as well, it may be because it is not drawing enough power. In that case, you may wish to contact Amazon to purchase a replacement cable for your device.

Link Your Amazon Account

The next step in setting up your device is linking your Amazon account. Your Amazon account will be where all of the purchases on your device are made from. Any books, products, movies, or otherwise that you purchase or rent from your device will be charged to whatever payment method is on your Amazon account.

To link your Amazon account to your device, simply turn it on and go to the "Settings" of your device. To find your "Settings" menu, toggle to the screen where your apps are shown. Or, you can swipe down from the top of the screen and tap "Advanced Settings Menu." Once there, tap "Link your device to Amazon account." You can then input your email and password associated with your Amazon account into the login screen boxes. Once you have, tap "Sign into Amazon." Your device will then sign-in and link to your Amazon account.

If your Amazon account is not already customized to the feature of your chosen payment method, billing address, and shipping address, you will need to set those up, too. The best way to do this is from your desktop computer. Go into your chosen browser, go to

Amazon's URL, and then log in to your account. Once logged in, hover your mouse over your account name. A menu will come up that includes "Account Preferences." Tap this option and it will take you to a screen full of settings and options which you can customize for your account. From there, you can go to "Billing Information" and "Payment Information." Under these two headings, you can select your chosen options and input your desired information so that your account is set up.

Register Your Device

From your device, go back into your Settings menu. Again, you can do this by either tapping the gear-shaped application button or by swiping down from the top of the screen and selecting the "Settings" icon. From there, go to the "My Account" option. Now, tap "Register." Once you are in the register screen, you will be walked through the process of registering your device to your account. It is important that you register your device to make sure that you receive access to your warranty, as well as to make sure that your serial number is associated with your account. That way, if anyone were to ever steal your device or if it were to be lost, it could be identified as yours and you could hopefully regain connection with it after it was lost or stolen.

NOTE: At the end of the registration process, you will see a button that says "Register." It is important that you tap this again as this is how you save your registration information. Once you have, your name and login information will be saved as the registered user.

Set Up Your Email

Now that your Amazon account is set up and your device is registered, you will want to set up your email with your device. This will support you in receiving emails to your device, as well as in being able to easily transfer information and media back and forth from your Fire HD 8 device to another device, such as your desktop or laptop. This will also synchronize your contacts and calendar applications to feature all of your personal information based on what is in your email address. Do not worry, only you can receive access to this information from the Fire HD 8. Your private information and the private information of your contacts and calendar will all remain secured to your device only. No one else can see this information.

To set up your email, go into your Settings menu once again. From there, tap "Applications." You will then see an option that says "E-mail, contacts, and calendars." There, tap "Add account." You will then see a selection of popular email servers that you may be signed up with. They include Gmail, Yahoo, Hotmail, and AOL. There is also an option for "Other" in case you are not presently registered with any of the aforementioned email service providers.

If you *are* registered with one of the aforementioned service providers, simply tap the option and log in as usual with your email and password. The device will then synchronize your email, contacts, and calendar applications to feature your information.

If you *are not* registered with one of the listed service providers, tap the "Other" option. You will be required to input some information such as nameservers and host information. For that reason, it is best if you do a web search on how to link your host with your device for email connectivity. If you own a private email address, such as "sample@yourdomain.com," you will want to look up the information for the server who hosts your private email address. This would be whoever you pay a bill to in order to have your private address, such as G-Suite or Vista Print.

Transfer Your Media

Now that your device is all set up from a basic standpoint, you can transfer your media onto it. This is only necessary if you have owned a

Kindle device in the past. If you have not, you can skip this step. If you have, however, you may want to restore all of your previous purchases and downloads to your new device so that you can continue accessing them and using them at your leisure. If this is the case, follow the following steps to set up your device.

First, you will want to connect your *old* Kindle device to your computer using the USB cable. Once connected, go to the "My Computer" folder and open up the folder linked to your Kindle device. There, you will see files of all of your documents and downloads from your old device. Simply click, hold, and drag them over to your desktop to transfer the files onto your computer. Once you have transferred all of your desired files over, such as books, movies, videos, photographs, and more, you can go back into your "My Computer" folder and safely eject your old Kindle device. After the computer confirms that the Kindle is safely disconnected, you can unplug it from your computer and set it aside.

Now, you want to connect your *new* Kindle Fire HD 8 device to your computer. Use the same method of plugging it in through the USB cable. Then, go to your "My Computer" folder and open up the folder that is associated with the new Kindle Fire HD 8 device. Then, this time you want to drag the folders from your desktop and into the Kindle folder. So, click, hold, and drag them over from your desktop. Once they are all done transferring, safely eject your device from your computer and then unplug it. Now, your files are successfully transferred!

It is important that you understand that your files may still exist on your old device despite transferring them off in this way. If you are planning on selling your old Kindle device, make sure you do a factory reset on it to remove all of your personal information, purchases, and files from the device. That way, the person who receives it next can easily input their own information and do not see any of yours, thus protecting your privacy.

(To factory reset your old device, simply go into the Settings menu, and then tap "Device Options." From there, tap "Reset" and choose "Factory Defaults." Then, tap "Reset" again to confirm this. Your device will then be completely reset. All of your personal and private information will now be wiped from the

device and you can safely sell it or gift it to someone else while maintaining your privacy.)

Chapter 2: Using Your Fire HD 8

Now that all of your initial setup on your device is done, it is time to start learning how you can use your Kindle Fire HD 8. This chapter is going to walk you through the process of becoming acquainted with your device, learning to navigate the hardware (physical device) and software (apps, games, etc.), and discover how you can get the most from your device. This may take a little time to learn, so be patient and give yourself some time to figure it out. If it helps, you may prefer to learn to navigate your favorite features first and then keep this guide handy to learn how to use the other less-used features when needed. That way, you can refer back any time to be guided through the process if need be.

Navigating Fire HD 8 Hardware

The first part of being able to effectively use your Kindle Fire HD 8 is to understand how the hardware works. This is the physical aspect of the Fire HD 8 itself. Your device comes equipped with a power button, volume buttons, a headphone jack, a microphone, a charging port, a camera, and a micro SD slot. There is also an auto-rotate feature that requires the physical device itself to be moved to adjust whether you are viewing in landscape or portrait mode.

The ***power button*** on your device is located at the top of the device on the far right. To power on your device, simply tap this button and then let the device power on. To turn your device off, tap and hold the button until a power off option shows up on the screen. Then, swipe the switch to turn your device off. You can also select "Restart" to restart your device from this power off screen.

The *volume buttons* are located on the far left side on the top edge of your device. To adjust the volume on your device, tap the left side of the button to turn it down, or the right side of the button to turn it up. If you have headphones plugged in, this will automatically adjust the volume in your headphones. If you do not, it will adjust the volume in the device's built-in speakers. If you have your device hooked up to Bluetooth speakers, this button will adjust the volume control on the Bluetooth speakers.

The ***headphone jack*** is located on the top edge of the device next to the volume button. Here, you can plug in any standard 3.5mm auxiliary cord. This can connect your device to headphones or speakers that are auxiliary compatible.

The ***microphone*** is located on the top edge of the device between the headphone jack and the charging port. This small hole needs to be kept clear of debris and should not be covered by a case or anything else when you are using it as this will interrupt its function. The microphone will only listen if you are in an application or feature where the microphone is required, such as in video calls, video recordings, or in your Alexa Hands-Free feature. It will not listen to you without your permission.

The ***charging port*** is located between the microphone and the power button. This port is where the small end of your micro USB charger can be inserted to either charge your device or to connect it to a computer. It is important that when you have anything plugged in here, you keep the cord free of any pressure by keeping your device safely placed on a flat surface. Excessive or consistent pressure on the cord whilst inserted into this port can result in the port becoming defective, rendering your device unable to be charged.

The ***front-facing camera*** on your device is located on the front surface of the device directly above the screen. This small circular camera is protected by the same glass that protects your screen. Still, you should ensure that you are keeping it free of scratches or dirt to ensure that its image remains high quality.

The ***rear-facing camera*** is located on the back surface of your device. It is the small circle in the upper-middle part of the device. Like the front-facing camera, it is also protected by the same glass that protects your screen. You should also prevent dirt buildup and scratches on this surface to maintain the high-quality resolution of your camera. You can toggle between front and rear facing camera features from the applications within your device.

The ***micro SD slot*** is located on the right edge of the device, toward the top corner. This slot can be opened to place a micro SD card which can expand the memory capacity of your device. You can purchase micro SD cards separately up to 256GB. Anything stored on this external memory card can then easily and automatically be transported to any other device simply by moving the memory card over.

The *auto-rotation feature* is technically a software feature, but it is prompted by the device itself. By holding the device upright with the power button toward the ceiling, your device will automatically enter portrait mode. When you turn the device sideways so that the micro SD slot is facing the ceiling, the device will automatically rotate to landscape mode.

Basic Features on Your Device

There are three basic features that you need to know about your device when it comes to navigating it. These include your quick Access menu, your App grid, and your Navigation bar. Each of these will support you in locating different features of your device.

The *quick access menu* can be located by swiping down from the top of your screen. This will cause a tray-style menu to come down, showing you the various settings and features you can access. These include, but are not limited to, brightness settings, Bluetooth and Wi-Fi settings, and the advanced settings for your device. You can also learn more information about your battery percentage, pending notifications, and Wi-Fi connection from this tray.

The *app grid* is where you can see your entire library of applications installed on your tablet.

This is found by tapping "Apps" on your home screen. If you have many applications, you may need to swipe up and down from the middle of your screen to see the different pages. Simply locate the application you want to access, tap it to open it, and begin using the application. Alternatively, you can tap and hold the application to drag it to anywhere you desire to locate it on the App grid. You can also hold one application over another to prompt the device to create a new folder for you to store similar applications in.

The *navigation bar* is located at the bottom of the screen. This bar features important navigation features such as "Go Back," "Go to Home Screen," and "Open Task Switcher." This enables you to either go back to the previous screen or application, return to your home screen, or switch between applications that are already opened.

Downloading Apps and Games

Downloading applications and games on your Kindle Fire HD 8 device are extremely simple. All you need to do is go to your App grid and locate the "Store" application in the Apps menu. From there, you will be able to browse any applications or games that are available on your device. They are grouped by categories and genres, but you can also use the search bar to locate more. Once you locate the app or game that you want to download, simply tap it and it will bring up an info menu. Here, if there are any purchasing costs associated with the device, you will be told prior to downloading the application or game. If you change your mind, simply tap "back" and you will not download the application. After the application is downloaded, you can simply go back to your app screen, locate the new application or game, and launch it by tapping on it. From there, you can begin using any features located within the application itself.

Alexa Hands-Free Starter Guide

Alexa is Amazon's built-in assistant that supports users in using Amazon devices hands-free. This mode allows you to have your device access applications, information, and other great things for you. It is particularly handy in helping you launch applications hands-free, making multitasking significantly easier. It can also brief you on information, such as by telling you what is on your schedule, what the weather forecast is like for that day, and what the commute to work will be like if you ask it to.

Using Alexa is simple. Simply say "Alexa" to wake up the device, then ask it anything you desire to ask it. The best way to learn how to navigate Alexa is to begin asking her questions and seeing what she responds to. Most things will have an answer, but some may not. If you are unsure, you can always say, "Alexa, what can I ask you?"

Here are some other questions you can ask:

"Alexa, what is on my calendar?"

"Alexa, how do you poach an egg?"

"Alexa, schedule an appointment for 1 PM on Tuesday the 19th on my calendar."

"Alexa, how many meters are in a mile?"

"Alexa, how many centimeters is 5 foot 9 inches?"

"Alexa, what does my day look like?"

There are also other questions you can ask Alexa, called "Easter Eggs." These questions are for entertainment and can make playing around with your Alexa hands-free application even more enjoyable.

Some include:

"Alexa, how many chucks could a woodchuck chuck if a woodchuck could chuck wood?"

"Alexa, who is your father?"

"Alexa, who let the dogs out?"

"Alexa, what is your quest?"

"Alexa, I want the truth!"

"Alexa, show me the money!"

"Alexa, party on Wayne!"

"Alexa, I'll be back."

"Alexa, who loves orange soda?"

"Alexa, winter is coming."

"Alexa, what's the first rule of Fight Club?"

Chapter 3: Reading and Listening

One of the main reasons the Kindle Fire HD 8 device was designed, and one of the primary reasons why people tend to purchase it, is for its easy reading and listening experiences. The Kindle devices were originally designed to make reading Kindle eBooks easier. Following major upgrades and expansions in the software and with Amazon, they were also designed to make Amazon Audible or audiobooks, an easier experience as well. These devices are optimized for great reading and listening experiences so that you can consume your favorite materials in the easiest way possible. On-the-go or while you multitask, you can do anything with the Kindle Fire HD 8.

In this chapter, we are going to explore how you can begin making the most out of your easy reading and listening experience with your new Kindle Fire HD 8.

Buying and Downloading Kindle Content

The first step to being able to read and listen to the contents on your device is actually buying and downloading it. To do this, simply access your Apps screen and go to the "Books" or "Newsstand" applications. Within those applications, head to the "Store" option. Here, you can begin browsing all of the content available to you on your Fire HD 8. When you find a title you want to purchase, you can easily tap the title for more information. Then, tap "Buy" if you want to purchase a single book, newspaper, or magazine issue. Alternatively, if you are in the Newsstand, you will also see a "Subscribe Now" option that gives you the opportunity to subscribe to receive ongoing issues of a certain newspaper or magazine. If you subscribe, you can easily manage your subscription from the "Settings" menu within the newsstand. Subscribing means that you will pay for each new issue that becomes available for your device, typically on a scheduled setting. You will see the exact terms prior to agreeing to "Pay" for your purchase.

If you are unsure as to whether or not you want to purchase a book, newspaper, or magazine, you can always view a sample of it. Simply tap "Download Sample" and a sample of the content will be downloaded to your device for you to view. If you like it, you can then purchase the full title or issue. If not, you can simply delete the download and carry on until you find something you prefer.

Reading Your eBooks

Reading your eBooks is extremely simple on your device. You can easily go to the "Books" or "Newsstand" application. From there, you will see the titles that you have downloaded. Simply tap the title you want to read and it will open. If you have been reading it already, it should automatically open to the page you left off on.

To ***Go to the next page***, you can tap the right side of the screen or swipe from the right to the left.

To ***Go back a page***, simply tap the left side of the screen or swipe from the left to the right.

If you want ***to read a different book***, simply tap the "back" button from the navigation menu and it will take you back to the Books or Newsstand application. If you do not see the navigation menu when you are reading, simply swipe up from the bottom of the screen and it will appear for you.

Listening to Your Audiobooks

If you have purchased audiobooks, listening to them is easy as well. Simply go to the Audible application and begin taking a look at your available downloads. If you do not have any yet, you can go to the "Buy" menu and begin searching for a book to listen to. Once you have, you can easily download it and then toggle back to the Audible application's main screen. From there, tap the book you desire to begin listening to and hit "Play." If you want to manage your listening, you can use the various buttons across the bottom of the screen to go back a chapter, skip back 15 seconds, play, pause, stop, skip forward 15 seconds, or skip ahead to the next chapter. You can also change the listening speed from 1.0x to 3.0x. Lastly, you can view a full list of the available chapters by tapping the three bars in the top right corner of the application. There, it will show you how many you have listened to, what chapter you are currently listening to, and how many more there are. You can also toggle between chapters from this menu.

Reading Settings

Because the device was specifically designed for reading, Kindle Fire HD 8 tablets have a great selection of reading settings you can customize to make your experience even more enjoyable. This includes synchronizing reading progress, viewing your location in a book, viewing your progress bar and page flip, and changing your fonts, line spacing, margins, and background color.

To ***synchronize your reading progress,*** simply tap the center of the screen when you are reading. From there, you will see a menu icon in the top left corner. Tap the "Sync" button and your book will automatically update synchronization across all reading devices for where you are in this book. That means any device you begin reading your book from will be synchronized to this reading page.

To ***view your location in a book,*** simply tap the bottom left corner of the screen. This will show you the *location number* which tells you where you are on this specific device, the *page number* which will show you where you are in the actual book itself, and the *time to read* which recognizes your average reading pace and estimates how long it will take you to finish your chapter and the entire book itself.

To ***view your progress bar and page flip options,*** simply tap the center of the screen while you are reading. Then, you will see options across the bottom of the screen that helps you flip your page. You will also see a progress bar that tells you how far you are into reading, and how much time you have left on both your chapter and the book.

To ***change your font and text size*** of your book, you can tap the center of the screen. Then, a reading toolbar will appear. Tap the button that says "Aa." Here, you can change your text size using the +/- options. Lastly, you can change the font by tapping the current font name (i.e. "Georgia") and then tapping over to your preferred font. This can allow you to choose a font that you find easier or more enjoyable to read.

To *change your background color, margins, and line spacing,* adjust them through the same screen where you change your font and text size. Here, you can choose your color scheme for the background which includes the options of White, Green, Sepia, or Black. You can also change the margins so that more or less text appears on each page. Then, you can also choose line spacing. This will dictate how close together the lines are, which may make it easier for you to read by having them either further apart or closer together.

Bookmarking, Highlights, and Note Taking

In your reading application, you can easily bookmark where you are, highlight your favorite parts of the book, and take notes regarding the book that you are reading. These tools can make reading your book even easier. Here is how you can take advantage of these tools.

To **bookmark** something, simply tap the top right corner of the screen. A bookmark icon that appears like a hanging flag will appear. This means that the page has been bookmarked. If you want to remove your bookmark, simply tap this icon once again and it will disappear.

To *highlight* something when you are reading it, simply tap and hold the screen over the word. Then, you can press and drag to select more text. An options menu will pop up offering you the opportunity to choose which color you want to highlight the text as. Simply choose your color and the highlight will be made. If you want to remove the highlight, tap and hold it once more. A small "x" will appear over the color you have highlighted this word or phrase with. Simply tap this and the highlight will disappear. If you want to view popular highlights that other readers have used, you can tap the menu icon (three dots) in the top left corner of the screen. From there, tap "Additional Settings" and then turn the switch on or off next to the "Popular Highlights" option.

To ***take notes*** about the material you are reading, you can easily tap and drag to highlight the text you desire to take notes on. Then, tap the "Note +" icon that appears. Now, you can type in your note when the keyboard pops up. Tap "Save" and your note will be created. To remove the note, tap the notepad above where the note appears. Then, tap "Delete." Alternatively, you can tap "Edit" if you want to edit the contents of the note.

Listening to Music

Kindle Fire HD 8 tablets are also great for listening to music. Doing this is simple. Go to the apps menu and then tap "Music." Here, you will be able to purchase and download music in the same way that you can purchase and download books. Then, you can view it from the main screen of the application. To listen to anything, simply tap the preferred title and tap "Play." You will also see the option to skip ahead or back or play or pause the song.

Watching Movies

Movies are great for the Kindle Fire HD 8 tablet. With movies, you have the option to purchase or rent the movies that you want to watch. Simply go to the Apps menu and choose the Movie application. From the application, tap the "Store" button. Then, you can begin browsing available titles. When you find one, you can tap the title to read more. There, you will see the options to buy or rent the title. Tap your preferred method and then simply check out. Once you have, your title will be downloaded and viewable from your Movie application. If you have rented a movie, you will see how much rental time you have left in this space as well. Once the rental is up, the movie will automatically be removed from your movie library.

Amazon Memberships for Inexpensive Reading and Listening

Amazon has created two great memberships to make reading or listening to your favorite titles more affordable. These include the Amazon Audible subscription for audiobooks and the Amazon Kindle Unlimited subscription for eBooks.

Amazon Audible is a monthly subscription service that offers you one or two credits per month, depending on your chosen subscription level. With these credits, you can purchase any audiobook available on Audible. You can also receive an exclusive membership discount off of any other titles in case you want to purchase more.

Amazon Kindle Unlimited also offers a range of free titles that you can download and read on your Fire HD 8. This subscription service provides you with many free books to read, as well as discounts on other titles in their library.

Both of these services help you receive incredible discounts off of audiobooks and eBooks. If you find that you are an avid listener or reader, using these services may be a great way to help you save funds while still reading all of your favorite titles.

Chapter 4: Customizing Your Settings

The Kindle Fire HD 8 strives to ensure that everyone has the opportunity to enjoy their experience in their own unique way. For that reason, there are many different settings you can customize to make your experience even more enjoyable. In this chapter, you are going to explore the many different ways that you can customize your Kindle Fire HD 8 so that you can enjoy a more personalized experience with your device.

Change Your Background

If you do not like the standard background that comes built-in on your device, you may wish to change it to a more personalized background. Doing this is simple. You can do it with any pictures you have or that you have taken with your device's Camera or any of the stock images that come pre-installed on your device.

Simply go to your Settings by tapping the gear icon in your Apps menu. Then, go to "Display." From there, you can choose "Wallpaper." Scroll through your photographs until you find the one that you like, and then tap that photo. Once you have, you can zoom in or out and otherwise adjust it to fit the screen in the way that you desire. Then, you can tap "Save." Now, when you go back to your main home screen page, you will see your new background picture.

Recommendations

Amazon displays personalized recommendations on all of its "Shop" pages based on your previous purchases. They can also be customized based on what you have told Amazon that you have purchased, anything you have rated while logged into your account, and anything that you have indicated that you liked. This feature can be great if you are looking to find new content to purchase or download that is related to what you are already consuming. However, some people are not a big fan of it. Alternatively, you may wish to customize the content more to see a more accurate personalized selection.

To adjust your Amazon recommendations that are available, go to your App menu. From there, find the app called "Amazon Application

Settings" and launch it. Then, go to "Home Screen." Here, you will see an option called "Recommendations." Next to it, there is a switch you can tap to turn it on or off. You can also tap the title itself to enter it and begin adjusting the information featured in your recommendations. By telling Amazon what genres or content you like most and removing ones that it may have automatically picked up based on your searches and purchases, you can customize what recommendations are displayed for you.

Show New Items on Home Page

When new items are delivered to your device by download, you have the option of having them show exclusively in the application in which they are relevant to (i.e., downloading a book and it becomes viewable in your Book library,) or they can show on the Home Page. Having them automatically display on the homepage can make locating all of your new downloads easier. However, it may also result in your home screen becoming overwhelmed with new content. If you want this feature on to make discovering your new downloads easier, or off to keep your home screen cleaner, there is a way to do that through your Amazon Application Settings features.

Remember, to access these settings, go to your Apps menu and tap "Amazon Application Settings." Then, go to the "Home Screen" option. From there, tap "Show New Items on the Home Page." If you turn this feature on, all of these new downloads will be featured on your home page for you to easily locate. If you turn it off, they will only be viewable in their respective applications or folders.

Change Home Page Navigation

One interesting feature that you can change just for preference is how you navigate your home screen. The standard setting for the home page navigation setting is to have all of your apps displayed on pages that you need to swipe vertically back and forth to view. However, you can also choose to adjust the settings so that they display in one long, continuous page. Then, you simply have to scroll up or down on your homepage to view everything. If you only have a few things installed, this may not matter to you since you may not have any need to scroll or swipe. However, if you have a lot installed, you may prefer to adjust this to make it more comfortable for you to find your applications.

To adjust this, head to the App menu and launch "Amazon Application Settings." Tap "Home Screen" and then go to "Change Home Page Navigation." From this menu, you will see the option to adjust how you scroll through the applications on your home screen.

Wi-Fi Connection

Unless you have the Fire HD 8 with cellular connection, you will need to connect your device to a Wi-Fi connection in order to access the internet and take advantage of your device's online features. Doing this is simple. To do so, go to your Settings menu by tapping on the gear icon. Then, locate the "Wireless" option at the top of the menu. From there, you will see the option to "Connect to Wi-Fi". Tap this option. You will be brought to a new menu that shows you all of the available Wi-Fi connections that are within range. Select your chosen network and, if prompted, enter the password for that network. The device will then synchronize to the network and be able to access Wi-Fi settings.

Note that if you turn on the Airplane feature, your Wi-Fi options will not be available. You will need to turn Airplane mode back off in order to access online features again. You can easily do this from your quick settings menu by swiping down from the top of your screen and tapping the switch next to Airplane mode to turn it "off."

Bluetooth Mode

Bluetooth is a great built-in feature that allows you to display shows on your Fire TV or connect to wireless speakers so that you can listen to music through a better sound system with your device. Bluetooth mode can also allow you to use Bluetooth headphones so that you can share, listen, or communicate through your headphones as opposed to through the device speakers.

To adjust your Bluetooth settings, go to your Settings menu and tap "Wireless." There, you will see a Bluetooth option. Tap this and you will be shown all of your Bluetooth information, including what your Kindle Fire HD 8 device will show up as on other devices, what devices are in range, and how to connect. If you want to connect to a device, simply tap that device's name on the list of devices in range and tap "Connect." This will then connect you to the device so that you can begin using it and controlling it through your Kindle Fire HD 8.

Device Options

Each device has built-in options such as time, date, backup features, system updates, device name, and more. If you want to adjust these options, input new information, or back up your system, you will need to know how to access and use this settings menu.

Begin by going to your advanced settings menu and tapping the gear icon. Then, tap "Device Options." From there, you will see the options listed above. Simply select your chosen option and adjust your settings as desired.

For backing up your device, make sure that you are connected to the internet and that your Amazon account information is properly set up on your device. That way when you back up your device, it will be backed up to your Amazon account. This way, if you ever need to restore it or you lose your device and want to restore everything on a new device, this can be done through your Amazon account.

Sounds and Notifications

The sounds and notifications related to your device can be adjusted so that you have a more enjoyable or customized sound. You can also adjust how notifications are sent to you, such as through setting a notification schedule or setting your device to Do Not Disturb, so that you do not receive any notifications at all.

To adjust your sound and notification settings, go to the settings menu and tap "Sound & Notifications." Here, you will see the opportunity to adjust settings such as what sounds are associated with your notifications, how loud your device volume is set to, the volume of your notifications themselves, and when you are receiving your notifications. Each independent setting you choose to adjust will feature their own set of instructions that supports you by walking you through the process of adjusting your sounds and volumes and making sure that your notifications are being received in a way that works best for you.

Keyboard and Language

If you are not a native English speaker and would prefer to have your device set to work in a different language, or if you want to adjust your keyboard to make it more user-friendly for you, there are some settings that you can adjust within your keyboard and language menu. This menu option is accessible through your settings. Once you access this menu option, you will see the following features:

- Change Device Language
- Keyboard Language
- Keyboard Settings (to turn on Swype feature, adjust auto-capitalization and auto-correct, etc.)
- Text-to-Speech set up
- Keyboard Color

Each of these features will customize your keyboard and language experience. Simply tap on the setting you wish to customize and you will be shown all of the customizable options and guided on how to adjust them.

Accessibility Features

If you experience visual or hearing impairments in your life, you can still use and enjoy the Kindle Fire HD 8 tablet. The device has built-in accessibility features that enable you to manage settings for your Screen Reader, Subtitling, and more. If you want to adjust these features, go to your Settings menu and tap "Accessibility." Here, you will see a range of features available to support you in enjoying your device.

Undoing a Customized Feature

If you accidentally change a feature and decide you want to set it back to "default" settings, you have a few options.

First, if you recall what the default settings were, you can go back through the steps of customizing that setting and set it back to the original settings. This might be the easiest way. If you do not remember what the original setting was, you may see a "Restore Default Settings" option, depending on which menu you are in. In that case, you can tap this button. However, this will restore *all* settings for that menu. If you do this, you will lose all custom features you have set, meaning you will have to adjust anything you have changed.

Lastly, if you want to restore all of your default settings, you can go into the settings menu and under "Security", you will see an option to "Restore Device." By tapping this, you will restore all of your settings on the entire device to default. Any customized setting you have in place will be restored, and your purchases will be erased until you reset your device to your account. If you are going to do this and you wish to restore your purchases, photographs, videos, and other media, make sure that you back up your device *first.* That way, you do not lose anything in the process.

Chapter 5: Security Features

Amazon strives to make their devices safe and user-friendly for everyone. The Amazon Kindle Fire HD 8 has many amazing security features that make it safe for every user, as well as family-specific features that can make your device safer for children if you are sharing it with your family. Accessing and enabling these security features is important in protecting your information, as well as supporting younger users in having a safe and enjoyable experience every time. In this chapter, you are going to learn about the features that can support you and your family in having a safe user experience on your Kindle Fire HD 8 device every single time.

Lock Screen Passwords

Setting a lock screen password on your device can protect you from having any unwanted user accessing your device. This is important if you do not want other users using your device, as well as if you want to protect your information in case your device is lost or stolen. With a lock screen password in place, it becomes more challenging for a thief to access your device and make unwanted purchases or otherwise on your account.

To set a lock screen password, go into your main settings menu. Then, tap "Security." From there, tap the "Lock Screen Passcode." Here, you can tap "PIN" if you want to create a 4 to 10 digit PIN using numbers only, or you can tap "Password" if you want to set an actual password for your device using numbers, letters, and special characters. Using complex passwords are believed to be more secure for your device, though it may result in it taking longer for you to access your home screen by unlocking it when you want to use the device. Which you choose is entirely up to you. Make sure you use one that will be memorable, however, as you do not want to become locked out and be unable to use your device.

If you ever want to adjust or change your PIN or password, you can always do so by going back to the same Lock Screen Passcode menu. Your device will now ask you to input your new passcode. Then, you will see the option to change or delete your passcode.

Parental Controls

Using parental controls on your Kindle Fire HD 8 is easy and allows you to have more control over how younger users are using your device. There are varieties of parental controls you can set, including setting a parental control password, as well as restricting or limiting access to various features on your device. Using these parental controls is a great way to make your device enjoyable and safe for younger users.

Parental Control Password

The first thing you need to do is set your parental control password. To do so, go into the settings menu and tap "Parental Controls." Then, tap the switch to turn it "On." When you do this for the first time, you will be prompted to make a password for your parental control feature. This is different from your PIN or password that you use to unlock your device. Make sure you set it to be unique so that if your younger user knows the passcode to unlock the device, they do not also know the one to unlock parental control features. Once you set your password and confirm it, tap "Finish." This will now be the passcode you use to access and control all parental control features. Again, make sure that you do not forget it.

You will use this passcode to turn off parental control features, as well as to provide access to applications or features that may be password protected when the parental control features are activated.

Restricting Applications

Once you have set your parental control passcode, you can begin customizing the experience of your Fire HD 8 tablet for younger users. The first thing you can take a look at it restricting applications. When applications are restricted, they become unusable when the parental control setting is "On."

The applications you can restrict include:

- The Amazon Store
- Web Browsing

- Social Network Sharing
- Specific Content Types (i.e. books, apps, etc.)
- Email, Contacts, and Calendar apps
- Camera

The option to restrict these becomes immediately available when you set up parental control for the first time. However, you can adjust and change these settings by going back into the settings menu, tapping "Parental Control," inputting your password, and adjusting the settings in the next menu.

Password Protecting Applications

If you do not want to completely restrict applications but you do want them protected during parental control use, you can also password-protect them. This allows you to password-protect features such as making purchases, connecting to Wi-Fi, and enabling location services. This feature is also available in the Parental Control menu from your Settings menu. The password you use to access these features when parental control is enabled is the same one that you use to turn off parental control.

Chapter 6: Troubleshooting Guide

As with all technology, Fire HD 8 tablets do occasionally have some issues that result in users having a poorly impacted experience. If you are experiencing anything that has your device acting strangely, restricting access, or becoming unresponsive altogether, this chapter will support you in troubleshooting your device. Some things are as simple as a glitch that can be reset, whereas, others may require you to go to Amazon to receive support. This chapter will help you exhaust all of your options before you choose to go to Amazon for support. Keep this guide handy in case you face any of these issues so that you can quickly fix them or receive the proper support to fix them.

Unresponsive Touch Screen

If your touch screen is not responding or is not performing the correct functions for what you are attempting to accomplish, there may be a few things going on.

Here is what you can try:

For a ***frozen or unresponsive touch screen***, reboot your device. Do this by holding down the power button until the "power down" option becomes available. Make sure you do not choose to restart your device, but that you actually completely power it down. Then, wait 30 seconds before turning it back on. If this is the result of a glitch, this should solve your problem. If it does not, contact Amazon Support.

For a ***touchscreen that is responding incorrectly,*** you can start by locking your device then wiping down your screen with a barely-damp cloth. If there is any dirt or debris on the screen, it may be inaccurately recognizing two touches instead of just one. If this does not work, you will need to contact Amazon Support.

For a ***damaged touchscreen,*** you will need to contact Amazon Support. They will be able to assist you in having your screen repaired. Be careful about using a device with a damaged screen as sharp shards of the screen may result in splinters or cuts.

Issues Purchasing and Accessing Content

If you have purchased or downloaded content and it does not seem to be launching, there may be a few issues going on with your content.

If your issue is with ***accessing the content*** you need to:

1. Begin by ensuring that your device is properly connected to Wi-Fi. Downloads and purchases require an internet connection. If your connection was disrupted during the download, it may have resulted in the content not downloading properly. If this is the case, you can reset your Wi-Fi connection or wait until you are

in a place with better Wi-Fi to download your new content.

2. If fixing your Wi-Fi does not work, try turning your device off and then back on. Make sure not to use the restart option, but rather, to turn it completely off. Then, after 30 seconds, you can turn it back on.

3. If you are still experiencing troubles, double-check to make sure that you have actually purchased and downloaded the content. In some rare cases, the purchase may not have gone through due to Wi-Fi connectivity or a glitch, thus resulting in the

purchase not completing properly.

If you are experiencing issues with ***purchasing content*** you need to:

1. Make sure that your Wi-Fi is connected. Again, if there is a weak connection, your device may not be able to receive a strong enough signal to complete the purchase.

2. Ensure your payment methods are correct. If your Amazon preferred payment method is inputted incorrectly, or if you are using a card with insufficient funds, you may not be able to complete a purchase. Make sure your card or payment account is linked

properly and that there are sufficient funds to complete your purchase.

3. Check your digital orders through your Amazon Account (this can be seen on Desktop from the "Purchase History" option in the Settings Menu.) The payment may have already been processed but the device may have not properly informed you of this purchase.

Not Seeing Previously Purchased or Downloaded Content

If you previously purchased content and you are not seeing it on your device, there may be an issue with your device being connected to your Amazon Account. If you changed your password or for some reason did not properly link your device to your account and register the device, Amazon may not have been able to restore your purchases and downloads to your new device. In this case, simply go through the process of registering your device once again. This will allow the issue to correct itself. If it does not, go into the Settings menu, then tap "Sync and Check for New Items." This will push your device to sync with your Amazon account and show you any content or new purchases that are associated with your account. It will also download them to your device.

App-Specific Issues

If you are having problems with a specific application, there may be a few things going on that are causing these problems. Here is what you need to do:

If you are experiencing issues with a ***new application***:

1. Check the reviews that the application has in the Store. It may be an application that does not work well. Applications are designed by third-party developers, so not all applications work efficiently on the device. You may need to download a different application if you need it to complete a specific task.

2. Close and re-launch the application. Sometimes, a simple glitch has caused it to stop working properly.

3. Check your Wi-Fi connection. Some apps require access to the internet to work. If you are not properly connected, the

application may not be working properly due to a lack of connection.

If you are experiencing issues with an ***old application***:

1. Check to see if there are any updates for the application. You can do this by going to the Store app and selecting "Available Updates." Keeping your applications up to date will ensure that they are working their best at all times. Note that if one application is buggy, it can cause other applications to struggle to work properly. Keeping ALL applications up to date is important.

2. Force close the application by going into your task manager from the Navigation

Bar at the bottom of your home screen. Then, launch again the application. This should fix it if it is buggy.

3. Wait for a new update or get a new application. If the problem is due to an in-app bug and there are no updates presently available, you can choose to wait for the update to become available (usually within 7-30 days depending on the developer), or you can simply uninstall it and choose a new application.

If the issue is with a ***preinstalled application:***

1. Check to see about updates. Again, if there is a bug in the application,

performing any updates will support it in working better.

2. Force close the application by going into your task manager from the Navigation Bar at the bottom of your home screen. Then, relaunch the application.

3. If the issue is with the Silk Browser, you may consider downloading a different web browsing application. This browser is known to be an issue for some people and it is easily bypassed by downloading a different third-party browser.

Battery Won't Charge / Won't Hold a Charge

If you are experiencing issues with the battery in your device, such as it's not charging or not holding a charge, there are a few things you can try before rendering the battery irreparable.

If your *device won't charge*:

1. Make sure that your charger is plugged in properly. Make sure it is all pressed in place firmly and that it is not loose anywhere.

2. If the cord is old or broken, replace it. If you are using a generic cord, the cord you chose may not be able to deliver enough power to charge your device. In

that case, you may be able to resolve the issue by purchasing a new micro USB cord directly from Amazon.

3. Make sure that you are using the wall adapter that came with the device. If you are using a different one, it may not be able to transmit enough power into the device to charge it. If you lost it, again, your best bet is to get a new one directly from Amazon. Make sure you choose the one that is intended to replace the Fire HD adapter specifically.

If your ***battery isn't holding a charge**:

1. Power the device off, plug it into the micro USB charger and into the wall and let the device charge for several hours.

Sometimes, the device may be extremely dead. Letting it go through a full charge cycle will help reset the battery and charge your device back up fully.

2. Consider replacing the battery. Devices that won't hold a charge may have a battery that has been charged too many times, thus rendering it unable to hold a charge any longer. Even rechargeable batteries tend to die eventually. Purchasing a new battery or replacing your device may be your best option. If the device is brand new, contact Amazon Support.

Forgot Lock Screen Password

If you forget your lock screen password, the only thing you can do to attempt to regain access is restore your device to factory defaults. If this does not work, you will need to contact Amazon Support to gain assistance in accessing your device.

The Device is Not Playing Sound

If your device is not playing any sound, there may be a few different things happening. Here is what you need to do:

If your device is ***not playing sound through built-in speakers***:

1. Make sure that your device is not muted. Go to "Settings." From there, go

to "Sound and Notifications." You will see a volume slider here. Slide it up to make sure your volume is turned all the way up, or up as loud as you would like it.

2. If you are still not hearing anything, make sure your speaker is not covered. Keep the bottom left edge of your device open so that there is nothing blocking it and potentially disturbing your sound experience.

3. Next, make sure that your device is not plugged into headphones or connected to a Bluetooth device. If it is, the sound would be coming through one of these devices instead. Unplug or disconnect your device from the alternate sound

source and see if your speakers begin to work again.

4. If they are still not producing sound, make sure it is not just the audio file. Sometimes, in rare cases, audio files may be corrupted and the sound may not be working within the file itself.

5. If you are still not receiving any relief from this defect, you will need to contact Amazon Support to have your device repaired.

If your device is ***not playing sound through plugged-in headphones***:

1. Prior to troubleshooting headphone issues, make sure your volume is at a

reasonable level to refrain from any sudden loud noises in your ears. These may cause damage.

2. Make sure your headphones are plugged in properly. Press firmly down and make sure that the headphone cord is plugged all the way in.

3. Make sure your headphone cord is not damaged. Check the cord for any wire splitting or other visible damage that may result in the headphones not working. If you see anything, replace your headphones.

4. Make sure your headphone jack is not loose. In some cases, particularly if there has been persistent or extreme pressure

on the auxiliary cord while it was plugged in, the headphone jack may become loose. In this case, you may need to replace the auxiliary report or switch to using Bluetooth headphones instead.

If your device is ***not playing sound through Bluetooth device***:

1. Make sure that your device's Bluetooth setting is turned "on."

2. Make sure both your device and your Bluetooth device are properly turned on and are set to the appropriate setting to discover the devices during pairing mode.

3. Make sure that your Bluetooth device is compatible with your Fire HD 8 tablet. You can view a complete list of compatible Bluetooth devices on the Amazon website.

4. Consider trying a different connection to see if the issue is with the Fire HD device or the Bluetooth device.

5. Contact Apple Support if your issue persists as they can walk you through the step-by-step process based on any unique information that may be coming up on your screen during the attempted pairing.

Wi-Fi Not Connecting

If you are experiencing issues with your Wi-Fi connectivity, there are two things that you can do to resolve this issue.

First, make sure that your Wi-Fi is actually turned "on." Sometimes, you may accidentally turn it off through the quick settings menu. Swipe down from the top of the screen and make sure that the switch next to the Wi-Fi icon is set to "on." If it is and you are still not experiencing any success, try rebooting your device.

If you are still struggling to connect, the Wi-Fi connection may be weak or nonexistent. In this case, wait until you are in a place that has better Wi-Fi. Alternatively, if this is your home Wi-Fi, consider unplugging your router for a few moments before plugging it back in. Manually resetting your home internet in this way can ensure that you bypass any issues specific to your internet.

Make sure your parental controls are off. If you have your parental controls "On" and Wi-Fi is restricted or protected by a parental control password, this may be causing you to struggle to connect to the Wi-Fi.

This should be all you need to do to repair any potential Wi-Fi issues. If you are still experiencing any, contact Amazon Support from a desktop or alternative Wi-Fi connected device to receive assistance in setting your Wi-Fi up.

Blue Hue around Edges of Screen

Due to the style of the LED screen that Amazon chose to use to create their Fire HD 8 devices, some screens may seem to have a bluish hue or tinge around the edges of the screen. This may be worse in some devices than others. If it is particularly troubling, contact Amazon as they may be able to replace your device. However, this is normal for this device and typically users find it is not disturbing during their use. Turning your brightness down a bit may support you in having a better viewing experience if you find it to be disruptive or annoying.

Chapter 7: Accessories

In addition to your device itself, there are several accessory options that you can choose to accessorize your device with. These options typically offer both convenience and safety for your device by protecting it from many types of accidental damage. Cases and screen protectors, for example, can protect against damage from dropping the device or scratching the screen. Other accessories include kickstands, which are a type of case that offers a support to hold the device up for you in case you want to view content without having to hold the device up yourself. In this chapter, we will explore some accessory options that you have for your device and what you should consider getting with it.

Cases

There are many case options available for your Kindle Fire HD 8 tablet. Different styles of cases offer different support. Furthermore, each style of the case has different designs which mean that you can customize your case for your own pleasure. Designs range from various bold and modern colors to unique patterns and textures that offer personalization. The design of the case is not as important as the style of case you choose. Each style offers varying degrees of protection.

Sleeve-style cases are a great solution for anyone who is generally protective over their devices but who needs some basic support when storing the device. These cases are designed to be like a pocket that your device slides inside of. This can protect it from dropping or scratching during storage. However, this case offers minimal support during usage.

Clip-on cases are the ones that offer the most all-around support. While they do not tend to protect the screen as much, these are the cases that have the most durable options. You can select ones that are simple silicone clip-on cases or ones that are hard plastic. You can also get ones that are made of a combination of a silicone slip and a hard plastic clip-on that provide maximum protection against drops.

Portfolio cases are a popular style of case that offers the protection of the sleeve when storing it, protecting both the device itself and the case from minor drops. They are also clip-on, meaning that the device continues to be protected even during use. While this is not as intense of protection as the clip-on cases, it offers more protection than what the sleeve offers.

Kick Stands

Kick-stands can be purchased separately or can be a feature of a clip-on hard plastic case. These are small stands that prop out behind the device holding it up. These features are great for anyone who may be using the device hands-free. It makes it easier to read, watch movies, or even check on recipe details when cooking. It can be extremely supportive to any hands-free experience or multitasking that you need to do.

Screen Protectors

The market is filled with many different styles of screen protectors. Choosing a good, high-quality screen protector and applying it properly is important. Screen protectors protect your device against bumps on the screen, as well as scratches. While they are not able to protect against absolutely all types of screen damage, they do offer a great support in ensuring that your screen is not scratched or damaged during use. They can also add an extra layer of protection for minor spills that may be exposed to the screen. It is essential to put a high-quality screen protector on your device if you want to save it from damage.

Conclusion

Congratulations again on purchasing your brand new Kindle Fire HD 8 tablet!

This handy device is incredible. From supporting you in consuming content and experiencing entertainment to assisting you in personal management, this device has many options. Taking advantage of all of the features available to you is a great way to ensure that you get the most from your device.

I hope that within this book, you were able to understand how to access and use features and troubleshoot anything that may have been causing you to have difficulty getting the most out of your device. By knowing how to properly use all of the features and how to troubleshoot various issues you may face, you can ensure that you get the best experience with your Fire HD 8 tablet.

Make sure you keep this guide handy so that if you run into any troubles with your device, you can easily refer back to it and fix the issue right away. That way, you can continue using your device with a seamless experience.

Lastly, if you found this *"Fire HD 8"* guide to be supportive and helpful in your Fire HD 8 experience, please leave an honest review on Amazon Kindle. Your feedback would be greatly appreciated.

Mark Howard

Check Out Other Books

Go here to check out other related books that might interest you:

Kindle Fire HD 10 Manual: The Complete User Guide with Instructions, Tutorial to Unlock the True Potential of Your Kindle HD10 Fire Tablet in 30 Minutes
https://amzn.to/2zVr3rq

Alexa: How to Use Your Amazon Alexa Devices New, Essential User Guide for Amazon Echo and Alexa (The Complete User Guide-Alexa & Echo Show Setup and Tips)
https://amzn.to/2NuBeFe

Kindle Fire HD 8 & 10 Tablet with Alexa: How to Use Kindle Fire HD, the Complete User Guide with Step-by-Step Instructions
https://amzn.to/2NMvarM

Amazon Echo Show User Guide: Amazon Echo Show with Step-by-Step Instructions, Amazon Echo Setup (The Complete User Guide)
https://amzn.to/2NOSdm7

Kindle Fire HD Manual: The Complete Tutorial and User Guide for Your New Kindle Fire HD Device in 30 Minutes
https://amzn.to/2AAuwMw

Fire Stick: Essential User Guide for Amazon Fire Stick, How to Unlock Your Fire Stick Like a Pro

(Amazon Fire TV, Amazon Fire TV Stick, Amazon Fire TV Cube)
https://amzn.to/2Mypamo

Amazon Echo Dot - 2nd Generation Amazon Echo Dot with Alexa: How to Unlock the True Potential of Your Echo Dot, Learn to Use Your Echo Dot Like a Pro
https://amzn.to/2KZ6VVL

Made in the USA
Columbia, SC
07 December 2018